THE SEDUCTION
OF TIME ET AL

THE SEDUCTION
OF TIME ET AL

William J. Russell

To order additional copies of this book, contact:
Xlibris Corporation
1-888-795-4274
www.Xlibris.com
Orders@Xlibris.com
24225

CONTENTS

William J. Russell—Retired from the U.S. Army Medical Service after twenty-four years. Mr. Russell has spent forty-three years within the medical arena. He has been teaching in one medical capacity or another for over thirty-five years; usually, in consonant with a medical, counseling, or nursing-type job. He has been teaching medical terminology at Mendocino College since 1987.

COMMENTS: If one thinks of poetry as reflections of our immortal soul, or at least, ripples in the waters of our deep unconscious, one may further intimate that these same ripples indicate something of the undercurrent of desires, impulses, and hidden idiosyncrasies of our personality that cry out for us to recall, spell out, or decipher. It follows then that we must view some of these self-made ripples in order to identify the underlying pressures of our own unknown. We may become better acquainted with our inner self to the degree that our mental health will also be improved; for, who among us can profess to know self to certainty?

Additionally, Mr. Russell worked for Mendocino County Mental Health from 1986 to 1996 as a quality assurance utilization review coordinator. This job brought him into direct contact with how the mental health system functions; and in particular, delving into the depth of client record keeping, a process that often revealed shortcomings in patient care, reporting, and compliance in treatment planning. Shortcomings in paperwork often equated into shortcomings of money received. His poetry, and often his teaching style, may relate his opinion regarding the dysfunction in the mental health field, and the frustration of one who has tried to make a difference. Today, in these sad times, it seems that mental health is still falling down, especially in Mendocino County.

ACKNOWLEDGMENTS

Gary Sheinoha of *Hemispheres:* "Thanks for sharing these. I was impressed by your work. 'Chariot Revisited' is a good parody of Emily Dickinson while 'What if Shakespeare had Written' is a fine imitation of his style. What a mimic's ear and genius you have."

Chris Hana of *Flume Press:* "I enjoyed the playfulness of poems such as 'Ecstasy,' What if Shakespeare had Written' and 'California Mental Health Tomorrow.' Images and details in these poems are surprising and fresh. And your Dickinson and Shakespeare diction and tone are dead on."

Rose Evans managing editor, *Harmony:* "Thanks for the chance to see your two poems for *Sea Fog Press, Inc.* I think that you have a solid poetic gift, and also some good values to share."

Genie Kester editor, *Infinity:* "Thank you for sending your work to Infinity Limited. Although we really have our space filled for about a year, I'd like to keep 'Legacy of the Damned' to try to fit it somewhere. Our satire board enjoyed reading that poem and agreed with you entirely."

Jane C. Schaul, Director Mile High Poetry Society: "We, at the society, have decided to publish an anthology of poems titled *Pierian Spring,* and we feel that your poem 'Legacy of the Damned,' will be a real asset to our book. Congratulations, William. Your work is, always, of the highest quality."

James Hedges, *The Camel Press:* "The Shakespeare spoof is interesting. I'm not sure it's 'great,' but it grabbed my attention: I can think of several women I'd like to send that to." Note to Howard Ely, managing editor, *National Library of Poetry* from C.S. regarding the poem "You Are The Seed of Now": "This poem is one of my favorites—it would be ideal for the *Sound of Poetry* album."

Judy Tarbell, Ridge Review: "Thanks for submitting your poetry to *Ridge Review,* it is *powerful stuff.*"

Lorraine A. Donfor, *Mind Matters Review:* "We accept all of your poems. However, due to the backlog, it may be some time before your work is published. Thank you for your excellent submission."

Lisa Hezel, *Hidden Springs Review:* "Congratulations. The fifth Prize of the Hidden Springs Poetry Contest belongs to you. Your poem, 'Infinite Touch', is vibrant, echoes beyond the verse and is well-deserving of the honor."

Cornel Lengyl, *Dragon's Teeth Press:* "Your poems, 'California Mental Health' . . . are timely, earnest, profound, original; they treat persuasively a most urgent and critical social problem."

Dan E. Weisburd, *The Journal (California Alliance for the Mentally 111):* "At long last I have received your writing and am thoroughly impressed. With your permission, I will hold it and use it as opportunity arises in future issues of *The Journal.*"

FOREWORD

Poetry, to me, is a language all its own; a symbolic tool that can be used to vent, in an abstract way, the internal anxieties, fears, and desires of the living of life. It is an expression of me as I am this instant. Using words, a language created by others, but putting words together in a special way that speaks for me alone.

Poetry is a form of escape, a grasp at sanity or insanity, a way to unleash a verbal turmoil in an accepted way (in our society). I may formulate problems, spin them around in my mind, even sleep with them, then behold—a poem is born. If I do this, then so must others.

Verse, then, is a way for man to speak of the realities for which no concrete referent exists. A way to capture a quality about something that words alone can seldom declare.

Poetry is an impression of the very act of living; another way for man to raise up on his hind feet and howl at the moon, to vent his painful separation from nature in cries and moans, to make love in speaking, and finally, to speak about his end and risk a guess at what eternity must hold; in all, a noble task.

The following is an actual excerpt from a commencement speech that I gave many years ago. The message still rings true today. As a nurse, I find these axioms most difficult to follow. I also have been told that reading the creed out loud seems to assist some with a feeling of well-being. Anyway, read on.

COMMENCEMENT
By
William J. Russell

Some say that stating a philosophy, in nursing, may predispose one's underlying biases. Just relating a philosophy may indicate interpretations of life gathered from many sources found inherently interwoven into a discipline, a science, or one's orientation to life, per se. Identifying an existing subjective philosophy, such as one produced by being in a nursing school teaching, may reveal a way of doing things common to many schools of nursing, a way of imparting a specific attitude, an ideology placing its catalytic grace upon the force of being stretching out before humankind, entangled within the moorings of time immemorial. This philosophy then becomes a byproduct of man's language in action, dedicated to the collective intellect of all that shall follow, founded on the knowledge of the past, and made relevant by the discoveries of today. It is always a process most resistive to the stasis of blind tradition; for all things change. Whatever the fundamental disciplines may have been, the philosophical metamorphosis that results should give clue to certain aspects of nursing that may otherwise go unnoticed, unheeded, or become lost, thereby leaving each person who has chosen to enter this place to gain their own foothold without the stepping stones of wisdom found and used by the many who have gone before.

The nature of man is realized in his unique ability to communicate, to be a time-binding creature, to gather his thoughts and cast them into the sea of knowledge, hoping that these many fragmented segments of life's experience will somehow take root, grow, and replenish mankind with new data to serve him, save and preserve him.

To this end I read you the following creed. It is a personal one that can be followed by all, not just the nurse, and a way of dealing with reality that has been a viable subjective tool in helping each instructor shape the graduate of today, an inner thought for now, a voice for tomorrow. It is an instrument of motivation not unfamiliar to the minds who reside here in this school, and for some, a way of life.

MY PERSONAL CREED

Give me courage enough to embrace a vision of the future, keeping my mind elastic to change, always seeking to learn, using my knowledge to aid in the healing of the sick and mending of the hurt or disabled.

Give me strength enough to stand fast against the eroding force of time; to keep myself healthy, strong, and able to move against our pathonomic foes, disease, misunderstanding, and ignorance.

Give me life enough to finish what I have started, so that I shall not shortchange anyone in need, and that I may have time to do the best that I can, in search of man and his meaning, here and beyond this mortal vessel.

Give me love enough that I may make peace with my God, as I perceive him to be, learn to forgive man, but never forget where I came or where I shall finally go. I am man, transcending the beast, out of woman, a creature with speech, one who has risen above all animal expectations. Though I shall challenge nature on all fronts, as man, I must be humble in the shadow of my creator, for in the end of life I shall be held accountable for my deeds done while living, be judged not by man but by a higher force, and leave behind a heaven or hell for those that follow, but in any case, I shall not continue in the form that you now behold.

Give me understanding enough that I shall be able to help those who wander bewildered in mental quandaries, give strength to those who need it in times of trial, and give faith to those who have gone astray in a world of confusing symbols created by man and his kind.

When all of these gifts have been satisfied, I shall then be whole, for it is in the giving of myself that my true realization becomes actualized, as serving humankind is both my destiny and my end.

AMEN

Having spoken these words out loud, I can never be the same.

THE SEDUCTION OF TIME

Eternal is the pressure
Of knowledge,
Fastening itself to an idea,
Clinging there, waiting
For man to discover
What he has
Known all along.

Everlasting in the force
That bathes
The brain of man,
Nourishing a notion,
Bringing to light
A spark of genius.
The gift that
Emerges in momentary
Glory from the dust of dormancy.

Never-ending is the ebb
Of time, playing
On the consciousness
Of man
Creating immortality through man
With language
Erupting from his throat of flesh
Bringing light to
Human thought.

Up from the fundament
Of the soul—
Time losing her virginity
To man,
That upstart,
Who must conquer all;
Then, with his greatest
And last triumph,
Man finally proceeds to
Do to himself in reality
What he has so far only
Proclaimed with words,
The aftermath of which
Is infinity.

CALIFORNIA
MENTAL HEALTH IS GOING DOWN

They say mental health is going down,
Opinion, wide spread, mental health is dead.
Budget to smithereens been blown,
Patients from the coup been thrown;
Casualties from which the blood is bled.

They say our service is just a joke,
I'm sorry, sir, but the system's broke!
So when it's in a crisis you've been blown,
And it's to another door you've been shown,
You'll have to wait there until you croak.

They say mental health is about to fall,
I guess the message is finally known,
For those whose minds with sickness blown;
We're not our brothers' keeper, after all,
We're just here to watch him fall.

PHOENIX RISING

They say California mental health is burning
From dust we came, ashes to ashes.
They say California mental health will have to crash;
Crash and burn before anyone will care.

State audit virus self-impelled,
Burn too, please do.
Your quest to strangle your host
Fails safe in fire white hot.

Phoenix rising in new form,
I doubt you worry too much,
Those who fell with you are barely warm;
But oh, how they felt the fiery storm!

THE QUALITY ASSURANCE DILEMMA

Dedicated, almost driven
        to high ideal.
In search of flawless fact
        of fleeting touch.
Searching for sanity in a system
        without same
Is like looking towards tomorrow
        to explain today.

Devoted, duty sworn,
        to elevated principle.
In a society where principles, per se,
        reside incongruently.

Dreaming, of values that could be;
        an idealism that suffers
        the anguish of paucity
In a climate of dys-concern.

Finally, succumbing to the
        order of things,
Because, to resist sameness
        creates undue pain.
Then, all remains insane,
        and the sun sets on
        the tranquil turmoil
Of finality.

HIS MYTH AND SEED

In all that man must feel,
And in all that man must do.
It must certainly be true
That he binds the two,
The feeling and the deed,
Together with his word,
And so perpetuates himself
With myth and seed,
Until he has met his organic
End indeed.
But this end is only
The beginning,
For his myth and seed
Will carry on the deed.

CALIFORNIA
MENTAL HEALTH TOMORROW

I heard a voice within my brain
It wasn't my own,
I would have known the sound.
It kept on saying,
In sick repetition, again and again,
Repeating things I dare not
       out loud expound.
My inner world, before me,
Like worms in a rain.

My panic came in bursts,
My acts, self-injurious, in spurts,
My blood in squirts.
A crisis, full blown,
A mind alone,
Then, you told me,
"Sorry, you're on your own."

OUR RULING ETHIC

Friends, countrymen, fellow Americans,
I am here to dismantle mental health,
        not praise her,
Let the indigent eat with swine,
        the cake is gone.
Let the homeless be without shelter.
The jobless without work,
And the mentally ill without care;
In God we trust, all others must pay
        their way.
Truly, a demoncratic era is upon us
And shall swallow us in swill
As we walk upon this wasteland earth
All the days of our life,
And to our infinite end.

LEGACY OF THE DAMNED

Steeped in bureaucratic tripe
The mental health system dwells,
Sick itself, limping in the streets
      of uncertainty;
An amoeba-like entity that
Falls prey to any sweet seduction.
While agencies take their toll,
Like cancerous lesions that strangle
      their host;
And everyone gets their monetary
      share, save for the sick,
Who wander like zombies
      in mental quandaries,
While paperwork mounts high,
A bloodless substitute for any cure,
And a monument to those who have
      silently succumbed.

INVISIBLE PEOPLE

They walk the streets at night in the shadow
    of their blight,
Unseen by the eyes that grace the day.
Each within their world of fright.
No help, no job, no place to stay.
Invisible people who share a society
Side by side with those of
    a false propriety.

They walk the streets at night in the shadow
    of their plight,
As they know not the day from night,
Mental images that melt at touch, and
    soul without organic clutch.
Shunned by those who see the light,
For fear that they too may lose the fight.

They walk the streets at night in the shadow
    cast by fear and false contrite.
Invisible people untouched by sound or sight,
Touched only by the plague of brain disease;
An unwelcome guest that will not cease.
While you and I walk the streets without
    a mental anguish, between us,
And pretend that our brother's care is
    beneath us.

DICHOTOMY

To be above all the restless turmoil.
To spread my immaterial wings and fly.
To reach the edge of earth and sky.
To be far away from soot and soil.

Two worlds have I, one here, another in higher place.
Two places in which to be, one here, another heaven spent.
Two directions am I driven without relent.
Two worlds have I, one in restless place,
          another with slower pace.

Too much this body clings to weightless soul.
Too often caught in clench of material ghost.
Too brief encounter with organic host.
Too often concrete reality takes its toll.

This reality, this world, this brain disease,
This schizophrenia, in exacerbation;
This melting reality that will not cease,
This plastic life, this internal aberration.

To-and-fro the pendulum of time is swinging—
To-and-fro my mind is bending—
To-and-fro the medication is blending—
To-and-fro my psychosis is unending.

INFINITE DIGRESS

One could be of infinite digress,
Never touching the ground of now,
Never touching the leaves of fall,
Looking away from the sunset—
Not seeing the colors,
Not beholding the universe,
Nor its unfolding;
Infinitesimally digressing into
A world of organicity,
A microcosm of self;
A schizophrenic place
That knows no time or space.

GENETIC PUSH

That love has often found me—
In search of material ghost.
Sperm, infecting egg with life,
That mortal host—
Imparting finite touch
To fleeting sinew.
Subservient to immortal soul.
So much of self invested
In mindless tissue,
With genetic push,
That time has lost her innocence
To organic creatures upon two feet;
And, sanity has been given to organicity,
A schizophrenic veil that covers
All that I can ever see.
Until death and I do meet.

SCHIZOPHRENIC PLACES

Let us gather up some sleepless nights
With paranoid visitations in hasty flights
Found in schizophrenic places
Complete with haunted faces
Demonic dungeons in tissue abide
On faceless neurons of minds tongue-tied
Where delusions play upon a tortured soul
Ranting their soundless rasp of malcontent
While therapies pointlessly interrogate
To understand a chemistry with words
Where words—at best—collide with words
While therapies insult and insinuate
So long as disease must here reside
That long their words not reach inside

I FORGOT

Forgetting protects one from self unveiled,
From ghostly encounter in unconscious space,
From things most phantasmal,
Existing in schizophrenic place.

Remembering is only for the very bold,
For others, dimensions left untold;
Rather, than in another dimension,
One might say, "Another demention!"

EMPTY FACIES

When I look into your eyes
Sunken amidst empty facies,
Otiose organs without an essentiality.
Problems projected back in troves.
Superficial words breaching the reality I seek;
Disguised as therapeutics,
Condensations to cool concrete pain.
But, it's all in vain,
Your therapies needed more
For self-inflicted aim,
Your chosen province from sickness born.
And though, duty sworn, you yet—
Leave me most forlorn.

S-T-R-E-S-S

Self-engulfed with
Thought where anxiety
Resides without hope of
Escape; thoughts, frozen in
Static placement not
Seen by those who look on.

WAS WITH THE WORD

To revere the symbol man was content
Many the verbal quandaries that confound
Behind man, a massive wasteland of wordy discontent,
And before him, great stretches of rhetoric abound.
Now, the coin of the realm, the word is spent.

To adorn himself with verbiage man was certainly proud,
His place in reality now most assuredly preserved.
Man, a time-binding creature since his speech endowed;
Now, the word, more powerful than man, becomes the served.
I doubt if the word will soon return the compliment.

WHAT GOES AROUND, COMES AROUND

Words of malice churn
Nefarious poisons;
Vindictive harpoons,
Like swallows, return
Instilling silent wounds
While wrath and anger burn.

SEMANTOPSYCHOSIS

Reaching, making one final verbal lunge
At an escaping thought
Sounds of man wailing
Against the salty winds of time
Rearing up on his hind legs
Giving vent to his fears
With audible cries to his peers
Sounds no longer recognized
By his four-footed cousins
Nevertheless, howls that signify
A displacement from nature
One that can never be changed
And the never-ending anxiety
In the soul of man
That must linger there
Since his separation from the womb of her.

Reaching, finally into the cosmic mind of man,
Into a portion untouched, by organic fabric
Into that force that is human
Yet not; then, realizing that this reach
Has grasped more than that which
One could ever hold—reaching no more
For man has been introduced to himself
And swallowed by an ever-increasing sea
Of his own words.

YOU ARE THE SEED OF NOW

You are what you bring to this moment,
Beyond the organic,
Very much the incalculable
Substance of being,
And in the process of being,
All that has gone before,
In whatever form,
And possibly all that will ever be (you)
You are the seed of now,
Germinating into tomorrow,
Maybe into forever.
You are a finite whisper
Within the great still—
Acoustics of the mind that only
The imagination can conjure.
You are the product of divine intervention,
Born with a soul, a body, and a purpose.
Define this purpose
And live forever;
Or cloud this purpose with doubt
And cease to exist, for then,
The viscosity of time shall
Engulf you without a single sound.
Gasp or whisper of evidence
That you ever existed at all!

MAN WAILING

I have heard of the sounds
Have made of the rounds
Have ridden emotions sailing
Have heard of man and his wailing

Against the winds of time
He has made a fine climb
While picking up a word or two
Before his life on earth is through

I see man looking up and rearing
Up on his hind legs and fearing
Against time's aging railing
His tale in moans he's wailing

Giving vent with his fears
With a great deal of tears
In a most audible
Yet—almost applaudable

Flow of squeals and cries
While saying his many good-byes
And it gives me a kind of ailing
To hear of his often failing

He's giving vent with a howl
From within his soft jowl
It's a tale of his separation
And of this you can make notation

It's from nature he's been torn
From her womb, not born
Now he cries like a babe
In the arms of a maid

One quite human and soft
Not most high and aloft
A beginning anew for man and his kind
A place on earth and in heaven he'll find

LIVING

The waning voice,
Once a distinct call,
Now only a seeking vacant whisper.
How loud you were last fall,
But, now you leave me like a lover;
Where have you left me,
The place,
The time,
Not familiar
At all?
Alas, but at the grave
I fear,
Forever.

PRAEMONITUS

ab imo pectore
fide et amore
ad infinitum
suum cuique pulchrum
amare et sapere vix deo conceditur

      Forewarned
From the heart
By faith and love
Without limit
Love is blind
Even a god finds it hard to
      love and be wise at the same time

AMOR VINCIT OMNIA

ab aeterno
ab ovo
a maximis ad minima
amor vincit omnia

      Love Conquers All
Since the beginning of time
From conception
From the greatest to the least
Love conquers all

MELODY AS CATALYST

Soft music sounds tilt the head,
Bring sweet memories from below,
Behind the human mask emotions ebb,
With steady and gentle tow.
Thoughts of dew glisten there,
Frozen within a mental web.
Then, with love's warmth,
Melt, dwell, and flow.

WHAT IF SHAKESPEARE HAD WRITTEN

Shall I compare thee to a winter's night?
Thou art as cool and certainly as dark.
Howling winds give an October fright,
And winter's lease hath far too small a mark.
Sometime too cold the mouth of nature blows,
And often is her disposition chilled,
Upon a heart already deeply froze.
Should by chance nature's quest be unfulfilled?
But thy eternal winter shall not fade,
Nor lose possession of that cool thou owest,
Nor shall death brag thou in his bed be laid,
When in eternal rhymes to time thou goest.
   So long as men can dream or wish for thee,
   So long lives this, and this says not to be.

CHARIOT REVISITED

Because I could not stop for love,
She lustily stopped for me;
The moment held us two
And immortality.

We barely moved, she knew no haste,
And I had put away
My past and future too
For her reality.

We flew together where few have been,
Beyond this earthly place;
We passed the seas of shining blue,
We passed the setting sun.

We paused before the edge of time,
At the acme of our swell;
Returning then, to dust we came,
Organic bodies homely spun.

Since then it seems a lifetime,
But each touch of her,
It seems to me,
Gives a glimpse of eternity.

ECSTASY

I like a look of passion
Because I know it's true;
Men do not fake tumescence,
Nor simulate a semen flow.

The eyes with blank stare gaze,
And this is petit mort,
Impossible to sham;
Wet droplets upon the body clung,
By heated fervor flung.

Sweet daggers passion dipped,
Into entrails embedded,
Tasting nectar of love composed;
Two chemistries entwined,
Exploding, mixing timeless souls.

SOMEWHERE ALONG THE FEMORAL TRAIL

In a dreamlike state
You can find me somewhere
Along the arching pectoral slope.
A night-veiled courier
Bringing warmth to coolness,
Turgidity to flaccidity.
And activity to dormancy.

In a dreamlike trance
You can find me somewhere
Along the mesial femoral slope.
A nocturnal emissary
Bringing light to conscious thought,
Life to stillness,
And motion to quietude.

On my somnambulistic steed
You can find me somewhere
Along the femoral trail.
A visitor into darkness
Bringing light to understanding,
Coming from aloneness,
Leaving separateness behind,
Momentarily.

INFINITE TOUCH

Yours eyes are lit like gems
And if I but look into them,
With a mind that numbly goes,
I should forget my name;
And your beauty bids me go,
From eyes to face,
And find my earthly place.

Your breasts are fit for pearls,
And if I but place them there,
With hands that quiver so,
I should forget my soul;
And your beauty bids me go,
From pearl to breast,
And seed my passion's quest.

Your lips are fit for fine wine,
And if I but place mine to yours,
With a heart that flutters so,
I should forget my place in time;
And your taste bids me go,
From lip to soul,
And seek eternity divine.

LOVE SILENTLY OR NOT AT ALL

To love aloud is very foolish,
But foolish more, I know,
To hold within the heart
A burning need to flow.

Who love, and others do not see,
Who hurt, and none observe,
Whose loving eyes no lover
Returns with burning gaze?

To love alone is very safe,
But safer more, I know,
To never loved at all,
For then, no pain to show.

TO BE LOVED BY YOU

To be loved by you
With tender haste,
Delicate as light rain falling
In a gentle breezelike spattering,
As if to caress from head to toe,
For so lost in this tender swarm, am I,
That separation is painful to the core;
For what has been loved in quiet lust,
Now recedes on waves of passion lost,
Until, on cresting once again,
My love for you seeds a desire,
Born anew, with you,
And, a wanting once again
To be loved by you.

NEVER, NEVER LOVE

Time is on my side,
As I recognize it so,
To flee and take refuge,
And reside, before I go

Within your corporeal beauty,
Sweet substance of escape—
Momentary transfixion complete.
Youth, in part, reclaim, agape

Vicarious reclamation, though it be,
Having residence in higher place,
Never touching material space,
Eternal triangle, ghostly chase.

ANTEROOM TO LIFE

From the womb to the table,
The flesh to the metal,
Away the skin,
Into the cloth.
The fading palpitation
From beneath the breast,
The inner spark—
Life on its own,
The blur, sensations
From without;
The within lost forever,
An eternity to wait,
To only, in part, return
And this life adjourns.

THEREIN LIES THE STING

Some chase butterflies,
While others run after bees.
I prefer the former,
Leaving the latter
To those who seem bent on pain;
A pursuit, I find most insane.

SPEAK UP PLEASE!

There are those men, who being of minimal
　　　　testicular fortitude,
Will never challenge another's words;
Allowing a suffering phrase to pass
　　　　without contention,
Not to mention, the often lingering platitude.

Being without certitude, seems fine,
On this they won't decline.
But the words of challenge will not come,
It is better to hide behind a phrase,
　　　　and then abstain,
Than to test the word face to face,
　　　　and chance disgrace.

WHAT'S A PENNY WORTH?

The other day was full of thought
I thought about the world
And how it turned
I thought about life
And all its pain
I thought about tomorrow
And all its doubt
I thought about love
And all its good
I thought about hate
And all its bad
Then—I saw a penny
Upon the ground
And I thought about
Its worth
I picked it up and
I thought some more
Until a man said,
"If you put it in this parking meter,
It's worth about twelve minutes."
And I thought
No more.

ALTERATIONS BY TIME

How insidious you are
Forever creeping up on me—
Making silent alterations
In the stuff you weave so well.
What havoc have you done me?
The image in the mirror,
The wrinkled sallow skin.
The graying thinning hair.
Friend and foe man too.
You've caught me by surprise.
Stolen my youth away.
But I smile a timeworn grin,
My memories live on within.

HELLO NURSE

Hello there, young nurse
All scrubbed in white.
I know you can't hear me speaking,
For I've suffered a stroke, you see.
What's wrong, young nurse, so clean and pink,
Though I've lost my speech, it's still me?
I know I don't smell as good as you,
But then, I'm only changed at night.

Hello there, young nurse,
All bubbly with youth and motion.
Why don't you speak to me?
I'm not dead, just frozen in place.
I'm here, young nurse, so pert,
Dampened in my own secretion;
Death may soon cover me with grace,
So a word would be a kindly devotion,
For while many attend to this naked body,
Few enter into its life,
They only enter the room, so white.

WATCHING

Watching young girls make last-minute adjustments
Before entering the boiling sea of people.
Watching young men, watching young girls.
Watching the slow ebb of traffic pushing back the
     curbs of gray cement.
Watching the buildings spill their contents into the
Streets of an ever-increasing humanity.
Watching the sun slide down a ray of light into an
     oblivion of darkness.
Watching that blackness not giving a dark damn where
     it placed its feet of night.

Watching the end of another day, the beginning of
     another shift.
Soon the evening nurse would come and pull the shades;
Removing from sight the outside life,
And condemning me once again to my bed of rumpled white.
Watching, watching the useless limbs before me resting
Amongst the hills of sheets and pillows, flaccid, dead.
Watching the spider building her web in the far corner,
The sink with its constant drip, and the door,
The glorious door—soon it would open and bring life
Into the room; then, the watching could become talking,
But, never doing.

I AM WHAT I AM

I am a very definite me,
And perhaps, you are a very definite you.
Probably, there is no other way to be,
To be someone else, a hard thing to do;
And, the same holds true for me.
Even though I try, I try in vain,
I find that in the end I am myself,
And with you it must be the same.
We are both stuck with a certain
            inescapable self,
All bound and tagged with a specific name.
It is hard to say which factor decides the real you.
The name or you per se.
Or, there might still be another factor too,
One that makes you this or that way.
But when all is said and done,
We find that we are no more than we,
A bit of seriousness and a bit of pun.
After all what else is there for us to be,
But ourselves, for what is done, is done.

OLFACTORY SENSIBILITY

Sensations imparted in an olfactory way,
Come out like children at their play;
Subliminal questions to be answered
                straight away.
Showing us behaviors not always seen by day;
But, always true to what they say!

OK CROQUET

A sideward glance with squinted eye,
A crack of sound, when
            object round, let fly.
A shout, a moan, when
            past the hoop
The ball has flown.
But only a game, play we,
Our mind, for the moment, free;
You see, it's all OK,
The game we play is, not life, per se.
Just croquet.

MURPHY'S LAW IN RETROSPECT

When things seem to be going right,
And you have been trying with all your might,
Beware your possible fate,
You may be behind the "eight"—
You've probably gotten the shaft,
And brother, it's not fore, it's aft.

MEMORANDUMB

That I'm often driven to anxious toil
Fast paced, pushed by unseen hands,
On paper put, words, verbal errands;
Chasing finality, my torch to midnight oil.

When others are set free,
And gone outside to play;
Sorry, I'll just have to stay,
I've been memo-ed, don't you see!

THE ELUVIUM LEGACY

Dust settled on a bust questioningly,
"Why do you stay so still?"
The bust replied,
"Because I'm only a bust,
    nothing more."
The dust settled more,
"But you are a bust, at least,
    that is something!"
"No," came the reply, "Just a bust."
And the dust settled even more,
Until a pile of dust persisted,
    ever more.

LOGICAL SEQUENCE

The force is begun,
What is this force in question?
On what grounds this deed defended?
Where is the beginning, where the end?
Who says, "It is begun?"
I question the power,
But understand it not.
What force greater than humankind?
The cause you say,
Then what of man?

In the image of immortality, his flesh,
From the dust of the collected,
The aggregation of the all.
Certainly this a joke,
From the all,
Of the separation and the combination,
From the fire and the light,
The day and the night.
The precipitation, the water's halo,
The divided elements of space,
Here the source, the heat, the still,
The cool and the living.

Into the cold, the brutal, the breathing—
Among the finite, the dwelling, the burning;
From the static to the dynamic, the flesh,
The heavy hand strikes, the air intake begins,
Oxidation, and then, that motion towards the end.

From the womb to the table,
The flesh to the metal.
Away the skin, into the cloth.
The fading palpitation, the spark of life,
The blur, the sensations from the outside,
The inside lost forever,
O' for the return.

Today is tomorrow me thinks,
A reflection the future knows.
What is done in haste and not in thinking.
Hear me now, before the point is reached.
In midstream the saddle prone to wetness,
Drenched failures, most wet remorse.
This repetition a lost entity,
Fluctuation without recourse:
The burning bridge that gaps the space,
The puff and all is lost.
The puff and all is lost.
The hand falters before the final knock,
Never again to rap.
In a dream it happened, not by chance,
In a world of symbols,
Waxen images that melt at touch.
O' we've met before, you and I.
Not by accident either, or should I say,
        quite by;
Quite by other forces I suppose,
Of libidinous forces that compose.
In what realm lie thee?
Where again to be?
Here now, stand me out,
No there, not the corner to pout.
Still please, that I may approach and touch;
But, alas, it shall never be as such.

THE IN-BETWEEN

The organism throbs with the beat;
It moves with a certain cadence,
Bathes in a euphony,
Is in step with every movement,
        yet alone in motion,
A conundrum of actions, still ones,
        dormant ones,
An entity of unrest, but of direction,
An object in pulsation.

The organism thrills in sympathetic oscillation.
The vibrations ever grow, the feelings still flow,
The stimulus and the response, the vibration
        and the reverberation, the flow;
And, what a pity, the outlet.

The organism swells to the sound,
Wave after wave, thrill after thrill,
        spill after spill,
In and out, in every direction,
Seeping through the soul
Like so much oil in charcoal,
But all is lost in the passing,
And none remains in the being.

The organism expels the rhythm,
Only a medium in response.
Neither a receptive object nor an end,
A sorry thing,
Just a mass of matter in the middle.
This is what we are, not an end,
Just a middle.

JULY

Bring your flaming chariots
      across my sky.
Heated with passionless push,
Scorching the ground
      beneath my feet.
Rays descending with
      carcinogenic scowl
Upon my skin,
If I dare to behold your
      scarifying embrace;
And, be returned to ash.
From dust we came.
To dust we go as skyward
      veil begins to blow.

THE SEA

The sea, like life,
Has tides that swell.
High and low.
The sea, like love,
Has peaks and valleys.
Ups and downs.
The sea, like time,
Pervades the soul
Into eternity.

GOING HOME

Down a corridor in time
A town is waiting there,
A dingy bar wherein a beer I could share.
Perhaps with a friend, or two, or more;
Or on a lake I could sail
To some far-off shore.
But each return brings
Only the pain of knowing,
One can never really be often going,
Back in time, in body or in mind,
For where you've been once my friend,
You can never be again,
Going home.

Along some future road
Memories of past will fade,
And as time brings along each decade,
The desire to return will often grow.
To return to that near-forgotten past,
With the hope of regaining youth's bright glow.
But each return only brings out what is known;
You really can't be forever going,
Going home!

END WITH A SPASM, NOT A BANG

I thought war to end man,
But passion seems more likely.
Our seed to destruction
May from our loins
Come in eruption,
And rather than war,
We'll go out with a spore.